Liz and Joe at the Festival

Liz and Joe Series

by Jennie Cole

Gate HOUSE

Liz and Joe at the Festival

Published in 2023 by Gatehouse Media Limited

ISBN: 978-1-84231-372-5

British Library Cataloguing-in-Publication Data:
A catalogue record for this book is available from the British Library

Author's Note

When the first *Liz and Joe* books were created, I had not anticipated how popular the characters would become. Beginner readers instantly related to Liz and Joe, and recognised the everyday topics from their own lives.

I designed them in a comic book style to appeal to a wider audience, and the colourful photographs have remained an important part of making sense of the stories and offering opportunities for discussion, especially for those with limited vocabulary. I hope new readers of the stories will enjoy meeting Liz and Joe too.

Thanks to Ann and Ian for bringing warmth and humour to the characters. The *Liz and Joe Series* would not exist without you.

Jennie Cole

It was an exciting day out for Liz and Joe.
It was the day of the local summer festival.

The event was also running a photo competition, which Joe was hoping to win.

Liz and Joe had just arrived and already Joe was busy with his camera.

It was a good location for Joe's photography skills.

The festival was in the grounds of The Abbey, near their home.

But Liz was feeling very bored watching Joe take photos and she really wanted to look around the festival stalls.

Watching someone else take photos was no fun at all for Liz!

I won't be long, Liz!
I had it on the wrong settings.
62.5 bpm

I'll try again.

Joe loved taking photos of places. He also liked taking portraits of Liz. However, Liz wasn't that keen on having her photo taken!

Joe was quite the photographer and was always looking for the best angle.

Liz had to admit, Joe was very enthusiastic about his hobby!

When Joe had finished taking his photos, they walked towards the area where the stalls were.

Liz wanted to pick up a bargain on the stalls and maybe a couple of gifts. On her way in, she had seen a candle stall and another stall selling second hand books.

There were lots of other stalls that were typical at a festival and all part of the family-fun day out.

There was a Hook a Duck stall. Liz was tempted to have a go, especially because there was a prize every time!

The festival had fairground rides to keep children of all ages entertained.

There was even a traditional puppet show, featuring Mr. Punch and his wife, Judy.

Everyone laughed at the Punch and Judy show.

People of all ages laughed at the slapstick humour.

Liz and Joe could have watched it all day long.

Liz and Joe stopped to watch the Morris dancing taking place next to The Abbey.

Inside The Abbey, musicians were playing. Some played guitars, one played a keyboard. Someone else sang into a microphone.

It was a good opportunity to sit down and Joe thought the musicians were really very good.

In one area of the festival, people sat on the grass and gathered around a band playing folk music.

It was Liz's favourite music and they listened to the musicians for quite a while.

People of all ages got into the festival spirit, listening to the music and enjoying the good weather.

When the musicians stopped for a break, Liz went in search of the jam stall.

The candle and book stalls could wait. She really wanted to buy a jar of jam!

Joe did not feel as enthusiastic as Liz about looking around the jam stall.

Joe knew it would take a while!

Liz loved looking at the jam and pickle stall. She loved making jam from her own home-grown fruit.

Liz was tempted to buy two bottles of strawberry jam and one jar of pickles.

These would definitely not be gifts for other people!

JAMS &
PICKLES
STRAWBERRY
JAM
PICKLES
JAM £3
PICKLES £3.50
MADE AT WOOD FARM

After all the jam shopping, Liz treated them both to an iced drink.

Joe really enjoyed the lemon and lime flavour!

Liz and Joe walked through the festival to find a quiet spot for lunch.

Liz packed everything away after they'd finished eating their lunch.

And that's when Joe had an idea.
I've seen the perfect photo to take!

Liz was not convinced.

But as they sat and rested on the grass afterwards, even Liz had to admit she was wrong.

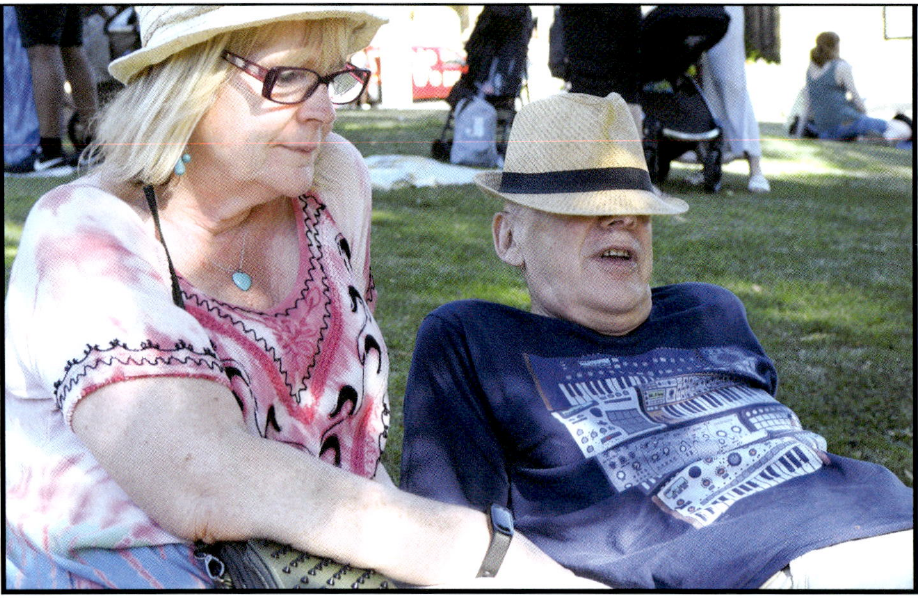

Joe had won the photo competition with his stunning shot of The Abbey against the blue sky.

Gatehouse Books®

Gatehouse Books are written for older teenagers and adults who are developing their basic reading and writing or English language skills.

The format of our books is clear and uncluttered.
The language is familiar and the text is often line-broken, so that each line ends at a natural pause.

Gatehouse Books are widely used within Adult Basic Education throughout the English speaking world. They are also a valuable resource within the Prison Education Service and Probation Services, Social Services and secondary schools - both in basic skills and ESOL teaching.

Catalogue available

Gatehouse Media Limited
PO Box 965
Warrington
WA4 9DE

Tel: 01925 267778
E-mail: info@gatehousebooks.com
Website: www.gatehousebooks.com